GROCERY STORE BUSINESS PLAN TEMPLATE

NEAL MORRISON

A startup business plan serves multiple vital functions. Firstly, it functions as a persuasive tool to attract investors or secure loans for your business venture. Secondly, it plays a pivotal role in convincing potential partners and key employees to join your company's mission. Most importantly, it serves as a navigational blueprint that charts the course for the launch and subsequent growth of your new enterprise.

The process of crafting a business plan is an invaluable opportunity to meticulously evaluate every aspect of initiating your business, enabling you to prepare thoroughly for a successful journey. This represents your moment to scrutinize any weaknesses in your business concept, uncover unforeseen opportunities, and strategize how to address inevitable challenges that may arise. It's crucial to maintain a high level of candor with yourself during this process, addressing potential problems with practical solutions rather than glossing over them.

A well-crafted business plan adheres to the principles of clarity and conciseness, ensuring that individuals from diverse backgrounds and industries can readily comprehend its content. It is advisable to refrain from excessive use of industry-specific jargon or terminology.

The majority of the time invested in composing your plan should be allocated to research and thoughtful deliberation. Document your research thoroughly, citing the sources of all information included.

Avoid making unsubstantiated claims or sweeping assertions. Investors, lenders, and other stakeholders reviewing your plan will expect to see realistic projections and anticipate that your assumptions are grounded in factual evidence.

This template provides comprehensive instructions for each section of the business plan, accompanied by corresponding fillable worksheets.

In the final section of the instructions, "Refining Your Plan," you will find guidance on how to tailor your plan for specific purposes, such as obtaining a bank loan or adapting it to particular industries, like retail.

Prior to finalizing your plan, it is imperative to conduct a meticulous proofreading, either personally or with the assistance of a qualified individual, to ensure it is free of spelling and grammatical errors while also verifying the accuracy of all numerical figures.

Business Plan

____

[Company Name]

Date:

Contact:

Confidentiality Agreement

The recipient of this business plan hereby acknowledges that all information presented by ___________________________, except for information already publicly available, is of a confidential nature. It is understood that any unauthorized disclosure or use of this confidential information may result in significant harm or detriment to ___________________________. Consequently, the recipient commits not to divulge this information without obtaining explicit written consent from ___________________________.

Should it be requested, the recipient pledges to promptly return this document to ___________________________.

____
Signature

____
Name (typed or printed)

____
Date

This is a business plan. It does not imply an offering of securities.

TABLE OF CONTENTS

Executive Summary

In your grocery store business plan outline, the Executive Summary is of utmost importance. Often, it serves as the initial section that potential investors or lenders review before delving into the entire plan. Its primary goal is to convey your enthusiasm for your grocery store concept and ignite the same passion in your readers.

Craft your Executive Summary as the final step, once you've finished the other sections of your business plan. This approach ensures a thorough consideration of all aspects of your grocery store startup, enabling you to summarize them effectively.

The Executive Summary should provide a brief overview of these key elements:

1. A concise summary of your grocery store concept (one or two sentences).

2. An explanation of your product offerings and shopping experience, highlighting the solutions it offers for your target customers.

3. Your store's objectives, outlining your envisioned milestones in one year, three years, and five years.

4. Description of your target market, defining the ideal customers for your store.

5. Analysis of your competition and what sets your store apart. Identify competitors and articulate your unique value proposition.

6. Credentials and prior experiences of your management team, emphasizing their contributions that give your store a competitive advantage.

7. Financial projections for your grocery store. If financing is needed, clarify the required capital, its distribution, and how it will enhance your store's profitability.

Aim to keep your Executive Summary concise, limited to one or two pages in total. After reading it, your audience should have a fundamental grasp of your grocery store, feel excitement about its potential, and express genuine interest in exploring your plan further.

Once your grocery store business plan is finished, revisit this section to craft your executive summary on the subsequent page.

Executive Summary
(Write after you've completed the rest of the business plan.)

Company Description

This section outlines the fundamental aspects of your grocery store. Include the following details:

Store Mission Statement

A mission statement succinctly explains the purpose of your grocery store. It can be a concise marketing tagline ("Fresh Harvest: Bringing Quality to Every Aisle") or more elaborate ("GreenGrove Market is dedicated to providing a diverse selection of locally sourced and sustainable products for a healthier community"). Aim for a statement of one or two sentences.

Store Philosophy and Vision

Define the core values guiding your store's operations. Principles like honesty, sustainability, community support, and quality products might shape your store's philosophy.

Describe your long-term vision for the store. This could involve becoming a go-to hub for organic produce, expanding to serve multiple neighborhoods, or fostering partnerships with local growers.

Product Selection: Outline the range of products your store will offer. Will it focus on organic produce, local specialties, international goods, or a blend of different categories? Clarify the niche or specialties that will set your store apart.

Customer Experience: Envision the ambiance and atmosphere you want customers to experience. Will it be cozy and welcoming, modern and sleek, or vibrant and bustling? This concept guides your store's design, decor, and overall feel.

Store Goals

Outline both short-term and long-term objectives, setting specific milestones to measure progress. For instance, if aiming for recognition as a leading organic provider, milestones might include establishing partnerships with local farms and consistently positive customer feedback.

Target Market

While a more detailed discussion follows in the Marketing Plan section, briefly introduce your ideal customer base. Highlight key characteristics like demographics, preferences, and shopping habits.

Identify the specific needs and desires of your target customers. Do they prioritize organic, locally sourced products? Are they seeking unique or hard-to-find items? Tailor your offerings to fulfill these demands.

Grocery Industry Overview

Offer an insight into the grocery industry, emphasizing what distinguishes your store. Discuss industry trends—growth, stability, or shifts. Describe how your store plans to leverage anticipated changes and trends. Address potential developments among competitors and detail strategies for successful competition.

Legal Structure

Specify your store's legal structure, whether it's a sole proprietorship, LLC, partnership, or corporation. Explain the rationale behind choosing this specific business form.

If multiple owners or investors are involved, clarify the ownership structure, detailing each party's share percentage. This information is vital for potential investors and lenders.

After reviewing the Company Description, your readers should grasp your store's mission, vision, goals, target market, competitive stance, and legal structure. Utilize the Company Description worksheet on the subsequent page to assist in completing this section.

Company Description Worksheet

Company Description

Company Mission Statement

Company Philosophy/ Values

Company Vision

Grocery Industry Overview

Goals & Milestones

1.

2.

3.

Target Market Industry/Competitors

1.

2.

3.

Legal Structure/ Ownership

Products & Services

This section delves deeply into your grocery store's products and services, expanding on the foundational details outlined in the Executive Summary and Company Description. Focus on the following aspects:

Your Store's Offerings:
Offer an in-depth overview of the products and services available at your grocery store. Detail the processes involved in sourcing, stocking, and delivering these offerings. Highlight crucial relationships with suppliers, manufacturers, or partners that play a pivotal role in meeting customer needs.

Addressing Customer Needs:
Successful grocery stores cater to specific customer needs or preferences. Clearly define the issues or desires your store addresses and outline the associated benefits, features, and unique selling points. While other stores may offer similar products, explain why your selection surpasses others—whether through superior quality, catering to a unique niche, or possessing distinctive competitive advantages.

Distinctive Elements for Competitive Edge:
Highlight any exclusive elements that give your store a competitive advantage. This might involve unique partnerships with local producers for fresh goods, special recipes, sustainable sourcing practices, or exclusive product offerings.

Pricing Strategy:
Detail your store's pricing structure, including menu prices, discounts, or any unique pricing models. Explain how your pricing strategy aligns with the market—are you positioned as a budget-friendly option, a mid-range provider, or offering premium products? Elaborate on how

your pricing strategy supports customer engagement and outline your projected profit margins.

Consider including additional details about specific products, store layout, interior design, or supporting visuals like images or diagrams in the Appendices.

After reviewing the Products & Services section, your readers should gain a thorough understanding of your grocery store's offerings, their relevance to customer needs, and the unique aspects that set your store apart.

Utilize the Product and Service Description Worksheet on the subsequent page to facilitate the completion of this section.

Product & Service Description Worksheet

Product/ Service Idea

Special Benefits

Unique Features

Limits and Liabilities

Production and Delivery

Suppliers

Intellectual Property

Special Permits

Product/Service Description

Marketing Plan

In your grocery store business plan, this section provides a comprehensive overview of your industry, competitive landscape, target market, and marketing strategies. It encompasses the following vital aspects:

Market Research:

Distinguish between research methods. Primary research involves firsthand information gathering, such as identifying competitors, conducting interviews or surveys with individuals matching your target customer profile, or evaluating foot traffic at potential grocery store locations. Meanwhile, secondary research relies on external sources like trade organizations, journals, newspapers, Census data, and demographic profiles, accessible from libraries, online sources, chambers of commerce, industry vendors, or government agencies.

In this section, elaborate on:

- The overall size of your industry.
- Industry trends, such as growth or contraction.
- The total size of your target market and the portion realistically attainable.
- Trends within your target market, including growth or decline, and shifts in customer preferences.

Barriers to Entry:

Identify specific barriers your startup faces and outline strategies to overcome them, which may include:

- High startup costs.
- Increased production expenses.
- Substantial marketing investments.

- Challenges establishing brand recognition.
- Recruitment and retention of skilled employees.
- Needs for specialized technology or patents.
- Navigation through tariffs and quotas.
- Addressing industry unionization.

Threats and Opportunities:

After addressing entry barriers, anticipate potential threats impacting your grocery store:

- Changes in government regulations.
- Technological advancements or disruptions.
- Economic fluctuations.
- Industry landscape changes.

Utilize the SWOT Analysis Worksheet to identify your store's internal strengths and weaknesses, as well as external opportunities and threats you aim to capitalize on or mitigate.

This section lays the foundation for understanding your grocery store's business environment, aiding informed decision-making and strategic planning.

SWOT Analysis Worksheet

	Strengths	Weaknesses	Opportunities	Threats
Product/ Service Offering				
Brand/ Marketing				
Staff/HR				
Finance				
Operations/ Management				
Market				

Can any of your strengths help with improving your weaknesses or combating your threats? If so, please describe how below.

Based on the information above, what are your immediate goals/next steps?

Based on the information above, what are your long-term goals/next steps?

Target Customer

Outline the profiles of your intended customer personas for your grocery store. Depending on your store's focus, you may target various groups, such as working professionals, families, or food enthusiasts. Develop demographic profiles for each group, covering:

Individuals:

Age range
Gender distribution
Location (residential area or specific regions)
Income level
Eating habits (like frequent shopping, occasional big purchases)
Food preferences (organic, specialty items, dietary preferences)
Frequency of shopping
Groups (e.g., families, corporate gatherings):

Group type (e.g., families, office teams)
Size of the group (small families, large corporate groups)
Occasion type (e.g., everyday shopping, bulk buying for events)
Shopping budget or spending patterns

Key Competitors

Recognize that within the grocery store industry, there are competing establishments and showcase your awareness of them. Provide a comprehensive list of key competitor stores, detailing their names and locations. Specify the range of products and services they offer that directly align with your offerings.

Clarify whether these competitors share similarities in terms of product variety, store ambiance, or pricing strategies. Highlight any unique aspects that distinguish your store from the competition.

Furthermore, acknowledge indirect competitors, such as big-box retailers or online grocery delivery services, which may not replicate your exact store experience but vie for the discretionary spending of your target customers. Explain how these indirect competitors influence the shopping choices of your customers.

Utilize the Competitor Data Collection Plan to strategize methods for gathering information about competitors in each category. This section aims to demonstrate your profound understanding of the competitive landscape and your plans for setting your store apart.

Competitor Data Collection Plan

(Competition name) – Brief description.

(Competition name) – Brief description.

(Competition name) – Brief description.

	Competition A	*Competition B*
Price		
Benefits/Features		
Size/profitability		

Market strategy		

After identifying your primary competitors, employ the Competitive Analysis Worksheet provided on the following page to conduct a comparative evaluation of your business in relation to theirs.

Competitive Analysis Worksheet

For each item outlined in the first column, evaluate whether you consider it a strength (S) or a weakness (W) for both your business and your competitors. Subsequently, assign a ranking to signify the level of importance each factor holds for your target customers, utilizing a scale from 1 to 5 (where 1 denotes very important, and 5 signifies not very important). Utilize these insights to elucidate your competitive strengths and weaknesses.

FACTOR	You	Competitor A	Competitor B	Importance to Customer
Products				
Price				
Quality				
Selection				
Service				
Reliability				
Stability				

Expertise				
Company Reputation				
Location				
Appearance				
Sales Method				
Credit Policies				
Advertising				
Image				

Unique Value Proposition (UVP)

Define what sets your store apart from competitors. Identify your unique selling points—whether it's offering locally sourced products, exceptional customer service, specialty items, or innovative approaches to shopping.

Positioning/Niche

Having thoroughly evaluated the industry, product or service offerings, customer base, and competition, you have gained a profound insight into your business's niche — that distinct and specialized segment within the market where you uniquely excel. In terms of positioning, you are strategically aligned to present your company to customers in a manner that underscores your unique value, setting you apart as the go-to choice within your niche.

Marketing Strategy

In this section, delineate your branding, marketing and advertising strategies for promoting your product or service. Advertising channels encompass:

Brand Development: Create a distinct brand identity that resonates with your target customers. Define your brand's values, messaging, logo, and overall visual identity to establish a strong presence in the market.

Online: Specify which online platforms you intend to utilize and explain the rationale behind these choices.

Print: Outline any print advertising plans, including publications or formats.

Radio: If radio advertising is part of your strategy, describe your approach.

Cable Television: Explain any cable TV advertising decisions and frequency.

Out-of-Home: Detail any out-of-home advertising methods, such as billboards or transit ads.

Marketing strategies may encompass:
Business Website: Discuss your website's role in marketing and how you plan to leverage it.

Social Media Marketing: Identify the social media platforms you'll use and your strategy for engagement.

Email Marketing: Explain your email marketing approach, including frequency and content.

Mobile Marketing: Describe any mobile-specific strategies you intend to employ.

Search Engine Optimization: Elaborate on your SEO tactics to improve online visibility.

Content Marketing: Outline your content creation and distribution plan.

Print Marketing Materials: Detail the use of print materials like brochures, flyers, and business cards.

Public Relations: Specify your PR initiatives and how they contribute to your brand's image.

Trade Shows: If participating in trade shows, clarify your objectives and strategies.

Networking: Describe your networking approach within your industry.

Word-of-Mouth: Explain how you intend to generate and harness positive word-of-mouth.

Referrals: Outline your strategy for obtaining and leveraging referrals.

Define the brand image you aim to project and identify the design elements, including your logo, signage, and interior design, that will reinforce this brand image.

Promotional Budget

Detail the financial allocation for your marketing and advertising efforts, both before startup and on an ongoing basis. These figures will be incorporated into your startup and operating budgets, respectively.

Utilize the Marketing Expenses Strategy Chart on the following page to aid in calculating the costs associated with reaching various target markets.

Marketing Expenses Strategy Chart

	Target Market 1	Target Market 2	Target Market 3
One-Time Expenses			
Monthly or Annual Expenses			
Labor Costs			

Pricing Strategy:

In this section, you'll delve deeper into your pricing strategy, building upon the foundation laid out in the "Products & Services" section. It's crucial to approach pricing thoughtfully since competing solely on price can erode profit margins for many small businesses. Instead, aim to strike a balance by offering competitive prices while differentiating yourselves through exceptional quality and service.

Alignment with Positioning: Your pricing strategy harmonizes with your positioning within the market. Recognize that pricing plays a pivotal role in conveying the value and quality associated with your products or services.

Competitor Comparison: Meticulously assess your pricing relative to that of your competitors. Understand whether your prices are higher, lower, or on par with the market norm, and explain the rationale behind these pricing decisions.

Customer Perspective: Acknowledge that while price may be a factor, it might not be the sole or primary determinant for your customers. Explore other crucial factors that influence their purchasing decisions.

Customer Service and Credit Policies: Outline your customer service policies, emphasizing your commitment to delivering exceptional support to your customers. Additionally, discuss your credit policies to ensure transparency and facilitate smooth transactions.

To guide your pricing strategy, utilize the Pricing Strategy Worksheet provided on the following page. This will help you make informed decisions that align with your business objectives and customer expectations.

Pricing Strategy Worksheet

Which of the following pricing strategies will you employ? Circle one.		
Cost Plus *The costs of making/obtaining your product or providing your service, plus profit*	**Value Based** *Based on your competitive advantage and brand (perceived value)*	**Other:**

Provide an explanation of your pricing model selection.
Include strategy info on your major product lines/service offerings.

Location or Proposed Location:

Existing Location (if chosen):
Explain the reasons behind your choice of location and why you consider it suitable for your grocery store startup. Highlight the following:

Convenience for Customers: Describe how the location caters to the convenience of your target diners, emphasizing accessibility and ease of visitation.
Parking Facilities: Provide details about the availability of ample parking for both employees and customers, recognizing its importance in enhancing the overall dining experience.
Proximity to Transportation: Assess the proximity to public transportation or major roads and how this affects accessibility.
Space Type: Clarify the type of space required for your grocery store, whether it's industrial, retail, or another category, and justify this choice.
Neighboring Businesses: Discuss the types of neighboring businesses and their potential impact on your grocery store's operations.

Location Criteria (if not finalized):
If you are yet to select a location, outline the criteria you will evaluate when making this decision, including:

Convenience for Customers: Explain the factors that will make the location convenient for your target customers.
Parking Facilities: Specify the parking requirements you seek in potential locations.
Proximity to Transportation: Describe your expectations regarding proximity to transportation hubs or major roads.
Space Type: Clarify the type of space you are looking for and why it aligns with your grocery store concept.

Neighboring Businesses: Mention the types of businesses you'd prefer to be near and those that might complement your grocery store.

Store Layout and Utilization
Store Layout Planning: Develop a layout that ensures a seamless and enjoyable shopping experience. Consider the flow of customers, aisle organization, product placement, and overall aesthetics to create an inviting atmosphere.

Space Utilization: Maximize the use of space to optimize both product display and customer comfort. Efficiently design aisles, checkout areas, and customer service sections while maintaining an appealing and functional store layout.

Distribution Channels

Outline the methods you'll employ to market and sell the offerings at your grocery store. These may encompass:

In-Store Shopping Experience: Explain how you'll cater to customers shopping within your store, ensuring an inviting and efficient shopping experience.

Takeout and Delivery Services: Detail your strategy for takeout and food delivery, including any collaborations with third-party delivery platforms to expand your reach.

Online Ordering System: Describe your approach to online orders, specifying the platform and technology you'll utilize to facilitate smooth online transactions.

Special Events and Promotions: Discuss any planned events, promotions, or discounts aimed at marketing your store and attracting customers.

Customer Loyalty Programs: If implementing loyalty programs, explain the structure and benefits to incentivize repeat shopping.

For established strategic partnerships or essential distributor relationships, share pertinent details in this section.

For those still finalizing distribution channels, utilize the Distribution Channel Assessment Worksheet to assess the pros and cons of each potential option..

Distribution Channel Assessment Sheet

	Distribution Channel 1	Distribution Channel 2	Distribution Channel 3
Ease of Entry			
Geographic Proximity			
Costs			
Competitors' Positions			
Management Experience			
Staffing Capabilities			

Marketing Needs			

Sales Projections

In crafting sales projections, you have a choice to draw upon actual sales data if your business has commenced operations and generated sales. However, if, like many startups, you are yet to make any sales, the process involves constructing estimates grounded in meticulous market research, proposed marketing strategies, and industry-specific data.

Develop two distinct sales forecasts:
Best Guess Scenario: This represents your realistic expectations, grounded in your market analysis, marketing strategies, and industry research. It reflects the outcomes you genuinely anticipate.

Worst Case Scenario: This scenario outlines a set of projections that you are confident in achieving regardless of challenges or obstacles. It serves as a conservative benchmark for assessing your business's resilience.

Throughout the development of these sales forecasts, maintain comprehensive records of the research and assumptions underpinning your projections. Future financing sources will require a clear understanding of the foundations upon which these numbers are built.

Upon reviewing the Marketing Strategy section, the reader should acquire a comprehensive understanding of critical aspects, including your target customer demographics, marketing strategies, sales and distribution channels, and your competitive positioning in the market.

Table: 12-month Sales Projections

Items	Jan	Feb	Mar	Apr	Jun	Jul	Aug	Sep	Oct	Nov

3 Year Sales Projection

	Year 1	Year 2	Year 3
Total			

Operational Plan

Within your grocery store business plan, this section provides a glimpse into the day-to-day functioning of your establishment, focusing on the practical aspects of your business operations.

Production/Operation:
Explain how you'll manage product supply, preparation and delivery, detailing the methods involved in creating and offering your grocery items. Provide insights into the procurement methods you'll utilize and estimate the costs encompassing transportation and labor.

Quality Control:
Detail the steps you'll take to maintain consistent quality in your products and services. Describe your quality control procedures, covering inspections, staff training initiatives, and mechanisms for collecting and acting upon customer feedback.

Location:
Offer a comprehensive overview of your store's physical location, expanding on the details provided in the Company Overview. Include specifics such as:

- Store space dimensions.
- Building type (e.g., standalone, in a shopping center, historical building).
- Zoning regulations or necessary permits.
- Accessibility for customers, employees, suppliers, and delivery services.
- A detailed breakdown of costs, encompassing rent, maintenance, utilities, insurance, and expenses related to construction or renovation.
- Information about utilities, including water, electricity, gas, and waste disposal arrangements.

Legal Environment:

Specify the legal framework within which your store will operate and demonstrate your readiness to comply with legal requirements. Cover the following aspects:

- Required licenses and permits, along with their status (obtained, pending).
- Intellectual property rights, like trademarks or copyrights.
- Mandatory insurance coverage for your store and associated costs.
- Environmental, health, or workplace regulations applicable to your store.
- Industry-specific regulations or standards relevant to your operations.
- Any bonding requirements, if applicable.

Personnel:

Define your store's staffing needs, addressing the following:

- Types of employees needed, including certifications or training required.
- Total number of employees needed, encompassing kitchen staff, cashiers, and management.
- Consideration for freelancers or independent contractors and their intended roles.
- Job descriptions for various positions within your store.
- Compensation structure (hourly, salary, tips, commission, etc.).
- Strategies for hiring and retaining skilled personnel.
- Training requirements and your approach to providing development opportunities for employees.

Inventory:

For grocery stores managing inventory, include these specifics:

- Identify the types of inventory you'll maintain, like food ingredients, beverages, or kitchen supplies.
- Detail the anticipated average value of your inventory, reflecting the invested amount.
- Outline your expectations for inventory turnover, comparing with industry averages.
- Highlight any seasonal fluctuations in inventory levels and your strategies for managing increased demand during peak times.
- Explain your lead time for ordering inventory and efficient restocking methods.

Suppliers:
Craft a comprehensive list of key suppliers, providing:

- Supplier names, addresses, and website details.
- Specify the type and quantity of inventory supplied by each supplier.
- Present supplier credit and delivery policies.
- Evaluate the historical reliability of each supplier.
- Anticipate and address potential supply shortages or temporary delivery issues, outlining your strategies.
- Explain if you have multiple suppliers for critical items as a backup plan.
- Address supply cost stability or fluctuations, and explain how you'll manage changing costs.
- Detail the payment terms set by your suppliers.

Credit Policies:
If extending credit, clarify:

- Industry norms regarding extending credit and customer expectations.
- Defined credit policies, including the amount extended and criteria for credit extensions.
- Process for evaluating new customer creditworthiness.
- Offered credit terms.
- Costs associated with extending credit and how these influence pricing.
- Policies for handling slow-paying customers, including timelines for overdue payments and when legal or collections agencies are involved.

Reviewing this Operational Plan should provide a comprehensive understanding of your day-to-day business operations for a grocery store.

Operational Plan Worksheet

Production/Operation:

Product Supply Management:

Explanation:

Procurement Methods:

Estimated Costs:

Quality Control:
Quality Control Procedures:

Customer Feedback Mechanisms:

Location:

Store Space Details:

Dimensions:
Building Type:
Zoning Regulations/Permits:

Accessibility:

Customer Access:

Employee, Supplier, Delivery Accessibility:

Cost Breakdown:
Rent, Maintenance, Utilities:
Insurance:
Construction/Renovation Expenses:
Utilities (Water, Electricity, Gas, Waste Disposal):

Legal Environment:

Required Permits and Licenses:
Status (Obtained, Pending):
Intellectual Property Rights:

Trademarks, Copyrights:
Insurance Coverage:

Mandatory Insurance Types:
Associated Costs:

Regulatory Compliance:

Environmental, Health, Workplace Regulations:
Industry-specific Standards:
Bonding Requirements (if applicable):

Personnel:

Staffing Needs:

Types of Employees:
Total Number Needed:
Freelancers/Contractors:
Job Descriptions:

Various Position Descriptions:
Compensation and Retention:

Compensation Structure:
Hiring and Retention Strategies:
Training Requirements:

Inventory:

Inventory Details:

Types of Inventory:
Anticipated Average Value:
Inventory Turnover Expectations:
Seasonal Fluctuations:

Strategies for Managing Demand Peaks:
Restocking Methods:

Lead Time for Ordering:
Restocking Strategies:

Suppliers:

Key Suppliers:

Supplier Details:
Inventory Supplied:
Credit and Delivery Policies:
Reliability and Contingency Plans:

Historical Supplier Reliability:
Strategies for Supply Shortages:
Backup Supplier Plan:
Managing Cost Fluctuations:

Credit Policies:

Credit Extension:

Industry Norms:
Defined Credit Policies:
Credit Evaluation:

Customer Creditworthiness Evaluation:
Offered Credit Terms:
Handling Payments:

Handling Slow-paying Customers:
Actions for Overdue Payments:

Management & Organization

This section aims to provide readers with insights into the individuals steering your business, their respective roles, responsibilities, and their prior professional backgrounds. For those seeking financing through your business plan, it's important to note that investors and lenders closely evaluate the qualifications of your management team.

Biographies:

Include concise biographies of the owner(s) and key employees. Detailed resumes can be included in the Appendix. In this section, offer a succinct summary of your experience and that of your key team members, utilizing a few paragraphs for each individual. Focus primarily on prior experiences and skills that have equipped your team for success in this specific business venture. If anyone possesses previous experience in launching and growing a business, provide a comprehensive explanation of these achievements.

Gaps:

Articulate your plans for addressing any gaps in management or expertise within your team. For instance, if you lack financial expertise, outline your intentions to hire a Chief Financial Officer (CFO) or engage an accountant. If your team lacks sales proficiency, describe your strategies for either hiring an in-house sales manager or utilizing external sales representatives.

Advisors:

List the members of your professional and advisory support network, encompassing:

- Attorney
- Accountant
- Board of directors
- Advisory board

- Insurance agent
- Consultants
- Banker
- Mentors and other advisors

Highlight any specific experience or areas of specialization within your advisory team that enhance your business's prospects for success. For instance, if your mentor possesses relevant experience in launching and growing a similar business, provide details of their expertise.

Organization Chart:

Construct and incorporate an organization chart that outlines both the roles currently occupied and those you intend to fill in the future. This chart should provide a visual representation of your business's hierarchical structure.

Upon reviewing the Management & Organization section, the reader should be reassured that your business is led by a competent and qualified team.

Utilize the Management Worksheet and Organization Chart on the subsequent pages to present your management team effectively.

Founder and Owner: 63

Name:
Ownership:
Qualification/Experience: [Provide a brief overview of your qualifications and experience.]

Name:
Ownership:
Qualification/Experience

Key Members
Role:

Name:

Qualification/Experience:

Responsibilities:

Role:

Name:

Qualification/Experience:

Responsibilities:

Role:

Name:

Qualification/Experience:

Responsibilities:

Gap

Advisors

Name:

Role:

Experience:

Name:

Role:

Experience:

Name:

Role:

Experience:

Organization Chart

[Provide a sketch of your organizational chart]

Startup Expenses & Capitalization

This section is dedicated to delineating the costs associated with initiating your business and the capital required for its launch. Please note that ongoing expenses after your business begins operations will be addressed in the Financial Plan. Accurate estimation of startup expenses is crucial to ensure you secure the necessary initial capital.

Start-Up Expenses:

By now, you should have collected most, if not all, of the required information during the development of your Business Plan. In this section, provide a comprehensive breakdown of your startup expenses, including a detailed explanation of the assumptions underpinning these figures. Describe the methodology employed to arrive at these expense estimates. If you have already secured loans or anticipate doing so, clarify the sources, amounts, and terms of these loans. Similarly, if you have secured or expect to secure investors, elucidate the individual contributions from each investor and the corresponding percentage of ownership they will hold in return.

Importantly, allocate additional capital for unforeseen expenses. Launching a new business often incurs expenses beyond the initial projections, necessitating preparedness. In the Start-Up Expenses template, create a category labeled "Reserve for Contingencies" and specify the amount to be set aside. While obtaining estimates from other industry peers is advisable, a general rule of thumb is to allocate between 20% to 25% of the total startup costs for contingencies.

Startup Expense	Amount
Total	

Opening Day Balance Sheet:

Utilize a balance sheet to present the anticipated financial status of your business on its opening day. As with the Start-Up Expenses sheet, provide a detailed explanation of the assumptions underlying the figures.

Personal Financial Statement:

If you intend to employ this business plan to seek financing, incorporate personal financial statements for each business owner and major stockholder. These personal financial statements should outline the assets and liabilities of each individual outside of the business, including their personal net worth. Investors and lenders often anticipate that business owners will leverage personal assets to fund a startup, and they will seek to ascertain the capital available from your personal finances.

Upon reviewing the Startup Expenses & Capitalization section, the reader should have a clear understanding of the capital requirements for initiating the business and the extent to which the business is adequately capitalized.

Financial Plan

The Financial Plan is a pivotal component of your business plan, and it holds substantial importance for lenders and investors who will scrutinize it in detail. Developing your financial plan serves multiple purposes, including setting financial objectives for your startup and evaluating its financing requirements. This section should encompass the following elements:

12-month Profit & Loss Projection:

Referred to as an income statement or P&L, the 12-month profit and loss projection constitutes the core of your business plan. To create this projection, please download the 12-Month Profit and Loss Projection template and input your anticipated sales, cost of goods sold, and gross profit figures (refer to the Sales Forecast). Subsequently, itemize your expenses, net profit before taxes, estimated taxes, and net operating income.

Provide a comprehensive explanation of the assumptions underpinning the figures presented in your P&L. It is essential to maintain detailed records of the methodology used to derive these figures, as this information may be required to address inquiries from potential financing sources.

	Jan	Feb	Mar	Apr	May	...	Dec
Income							
Sales							
Cost of Goods Sold							
Gross Profit							

	Jan	Feb	Mar	Apr	May	...	Dec
Expense							
Payroll							
Rent							
Utilities							
Insurance							
Advertising							
Total Expense							

	Jan	Feb	Mar	Apr	May	...	Dec
Net Profit							

Optional: 3-year Profit & Loss Projection:

While not mandatory for a business plan, a three-year profit and loss projection can be beneficial if you anticipate significant financial alterations beyond the initial year or if investors or lenders stipulate its inclusion. Utilize the 3-Year Profit and Loss Projection template to construct this projection if deemed necessary.

Table: 3 Year Profit & Loss Projection:

	Year 1	Year 2	Year 3
Income			
Sales			
Cost of Goods Sold			
Gross Profit			

Expense			
Payroll			
Rent			
Utilities			
Insurance			
Advertising			
Total Expense			

Net Profit			

Cash Flow Projection:

The cash flow statement tracks the amount of cash available to your business at any given point. Once your business is operational, keeping a close eye on your cash flow statement is imperative.

However, at this stage, you are crafting a cash flow projection, akin to a forecast for your business checking account.

Consider the cash flow projection as a tool to anticipate your business's financial transactions. It details when cash will be expended for purposes such as inventory acquisition, rent, and payroll, in contrast to when revenue is expected from customers and clients. This projection considers factors such as sales, inventory purchases, and payment collection schedules to assist in budgeting for upcoming expenditures and ensuring sufficient liquidity.

To create your cash flow projection, Use the 12-Month Cash Flow Statement template and follow the provided guidelines.

Cash Flow	Year 1	Year 2	Year 3
Cash Received			
Cash From Operation			
Sales			
Receivable			
Subtotal			

Additional Cash Received			
Sales Tax			
Rental Income			
Subtotal			

Expense			
Operation Cost			
Bills			
Cash Spent			
Subtotal			

Net Cash Flow			
Cash Balance			

Optional: 3-year Cash Flow Statement:

Depending on your specific requirements and the purpose of your business plan, you may choose to incorporate a 3-year cash flow statement. If deemed necessary, utilize the 3-Year Cash Flow Statement template to generate these projections. This document, while simpler than the 12-month cash flow statement, can still be valuable for strategic planning.

Projected Balance Sheet:

A balance sheet calculates the owner's equity by subtracting a company's liabilities from its assets. You have previously constructed an opening day balance sheet in Section 1. Now, download the Balance Sheet (Projected) template to formulate a projected balance sheet. This sheet will showcase the estimated financial position of your business at the conclusion of its inaugural year.

The primary distinction between the two balance sheets is that the projected balance sheet incorporates owner's equity resulting from the business's first year of operation. Lenders and investors may require this projection to evaluate your business's financial outlook.

Upon reviewing the Financial Plan section, readers should gain a comprehensive understanding of your financial goals, projections, and the capital necessary for your startup's successful initiation.

Balance Sheet	Year 1	Year 2	Year 3
ASSET			
Current Asset			
Cash			
Account Recievable			
Inventory			
Others			
Total Current Asset			

Long Term Asset	Year 1	Year 2	Year 3
Long Term Asset			
Long term Asset			
Accumulated Depreciation			
Total Long Term Asset			
TOTAL ASSET			

LIABILITIES	Year 1	Year 2	Year 3
LIABILITIES			
Account Payable			
Bills			
Cash Spent			
TOTAL LIABILITIES			

Paid In/ Invested Capital			

Earning			
Total Capital			
Net Cash Flow			
Net Worth			

Break-even Analysis:

The break-even analysis serves as a tool to project the necessary sales volume required to cover your operational costs, ultimately pinpointing the point at which your business becomes financially self-sustaining. To perform this analysis, kindly access the Break-Even Analysis template. Within this template, employ your profit and loss projections to input the expected figures for both fixed and variable costs. Feel free to customize the categories to align with the specific characteristics of your business.

Consider the possibility of creating multiple break-even analyses for diverse scenarios. For instance, if your labor costs fluctuate based on whether you opt for full-time employees or independent contractors, crafting various break-even analyses can facilitate a more informed decision-making process.

Capital Allocation:

In the event that you intend to utilize your business plan to secure financing from lenders or investors, it is imperative to provide a comprehensive breakdown of how you plan to allocate the capital acquired and the anticipated outcomes. For instance, you may allocate the funds to procure new equipment with the expectation of doubling your production capacity.

Upon reviewing the Financial Plan section, readers should possess a deep comprehension of the underlying assumptions governing your financial projections, empowering them to assess the realism of these projections.

Refining Your Plan:

Tailor your business plan to align with your specific requirements, target audience, and industry nuances. Here are some guidelines to assist you in this process:

For Raising Capital from Bankers:

Bankers are primarily concerned with your ability to repay the loan. When preparing the business plan for bankers or other lenders, ensure you include the following:

- The precise amount of funding you are seeking.
- A detailed breakdown of how you intend to utilize the borrowed funds.
- Explain how this injection of capital will enhance the overall financial stability and growth prospects of your business.
- Specify the repayment terms you are requesting, including the number of years required for repayment.
- Provide information regarding any collateral you can offer as security for the loan, along with a comprehensive list of any existing liens against this collateral.

For Raising Capital from Investors:

Investors typically seek substantial growth opportunities and anticipate sharing in the profits. When crafting the business plan for potential investors, make sure to incorporate the following elements:

- Outline the short-term and medium-term investment amounts required.
- Clarify how you intend to allocate the investment and illustrate how these funds will propel your business towards growth and success.
- Provide an estimate of the return on investment that investors can anticipate.

- Describe your exit strategy for investors, whether it involves a buyback, sale, or initial public offering (IPO).
- Specify the percentage of ownership that you are willing to offer to investors.
- Highlight any specific milestones or conditions that you are prepared to accept in collaboration with investors.
- Detail the financial reporting you will provide to keep investors informed.
- Address the level of involvement that investors can expect to have on the board or within the management of the company.

For a Service Business:

When developing a business plan for a service-based enterprise, consider the following key aspects:

- Pricing Strategy: Elaborate on your pricing structure and the methodologies employed to determine service charges.
- Service Delivery Systems: Describe the systems and processes you will implement to ensure the consistent and reliable delivery of your services.
- Quality Control Measures: Outline the quality control procedures you will have in place to maintain high service standards and meet client expectations.
- Employee Productivity: Specify how you will measure and monitor employee productivity to optimize service efficiency.
- Subcontracting Strategy: If applicable, detail any plans to subcontract work to other businesses. Indicate the percentage of work that may be subcontracted and whether it will generate a profit.
- Credit and Payment Policies: Explain your policies and procedures regarding client credit, payment terms, and collections processes.

- Client Retention: Describe your strategies for maintaining a loyal client base, securing long-term contracts, and fostering ongoing customer relationships.
- Expansion: If you are planning to introduce new services or expand your service offerings in the future, provide insights into these developments and how they align with your business's growth strategy.

By customizing your business plan to meet these distinct requirements, you can effectively communicate your business's value proposition and financial outlook to the respective audience of bankers or investors.

Now That You're (Almost) done) remember to go back, and complete the Executive Summary.

How to Attract Investors

Attracting investors is a multifaceted endeavor that demands a strategic approach. The foundation of this process lies in crafting a comprehensive and convincing business plan. This plan should not only outline your business model but also demonstrate a clear understanding of the market, competitors, and potential challenges. Investors are keen on businesses that exhibit a well-defined path to profitability and growth. It's imperative to showcase a unique value proposition, emphasizing what sets your business apart from the competition, be it an innovative product, cutting-edge technology, or a unique brand identity.

A key element in attracting investors is assembling a robust and competent team. Investors often invest in people as much as they invest in ideas. Therefore, curating a team with a blend of expertise, industry knowledge, and a track record of success can significantly bolster investor confidence. Highlighting the commitment and passion of your team members in your pitch can also go a long way in building trust.

Investors are inherently risk-averse, so market validation becomes a pivotal aspect. Demonstrating that there is a genuine demand for your product or service is crucial. This can be achieved by providing tangible evidence of customer interest, early sales figures, or partnerships with reputable organizations. Investors want assurance that their capital is being deployed in a business that has the potential to scale and yield significant returns.

The financial aspect is equally vital. Prepare realistic and well-supported financial projections that clearly illustrate the revenue potential and profitability of your business. Transparency is key here; investors appreciate entrepreneurs who are upfront about their assumptions and calculations. Additionally, it's essential to outline a clear path to exit, allowing investors to understand how and when they can realize returns on their investment, whether it's through an acquisition, IPO, or dividends.

These strategies, along with networking, effective pitching, and leveraging online platforms, can form a robust framework for attracting investors. Moreover, maintaining open communication, seeking mentorship, and ensuring compatibility with potential investors' values and objectives contribute to building trust and fostering successful investor partnerships. It's important to remember that attracting investors is a dynamic and ongoing process, requiring adaptability and perseverance to secure the right support for your business's growth and success.

www.ingramcontent.com/pod-product-compliance
Lightning Source LLC
Chambersburg PA
CBHW061002260726
48661CB00005B/2003